Things to Know About Venture Debt

First published by Kjøller 2023

Table of Contents

Introduction

Venture debt is a specialized form of financing for startups that has become increasingly popular in recent years. While venture capital funds get most of the attention, venture debt can be a valuable tool for companies looking to fund growth and manage their cash flow. However, it can also be complex and confusing, with many unique terms and concepts.

This book aims to demystify venture debt by providing a comprehensive glossary of key terms and definitions. Whether you're a startup founder, investor, or simply interested in learning more about this topic, this book will provide a clear and concise overview of venture debt and its various components. From interest rates and covenants to warrants and amortization schedules, each term is defined in simple language without any jargon, making it accessible to anyone. So whether you're just starting out or are already familiar with the world of venture debt, this book is the perfect resource for understanding this important and fast-growing aspect of startup financing.

Accordion feature

a term used in venture debt to describe a flexible line of credit that can be expanded or reduced based on the borrower's needs. The accordion feature allows borrowers to access additional funds as their business grows or reduce their debt as their cash flow shrinks.

Accrued Interest

This is the interest that has accumulated on a loan but has not yet been paid. It is added to the outstanding principal amount of the loan and must be paid along with the principal.

Acquisition Financing

This refers to the use of venture debt to finance the acquisition of assets or companies. The debt might be used to pay for a portion of the purchase price or for working capital to integrate the acquired assets.

Adjustable Interest Rate

This is a type of interest rate where the rate can vary based on a specified index or benchmark. In venture debt, the rate might be tied to the prime rate or LIBOR.

Advance Rates

This is the percentage of the value of the assets that can be borrowed using asset-based lending. Higher advance rates are more favorable to the borrower as they can borrow more money with the same amount of collateral.

Advancement

a term used in venture debt to describe the initial disbursement of funds to a borrower. These funds are typically used to finance working capital, purchase inventory, or hire employees. Advancements may also be called tranches or drawdowns.

Affirmative Covenants

These are contractual requirements that the borrower must fulfill, such as maintaining certain financial ratios, providing regular financial statements, or obtaining approval from the lender before taking certain actions.

Altman Z-score

a formula used to predict the likelihood of a company's bankruptcy. Venture debt lenders may use the Altman Z-score to assess the creditworthiness of potential borrowers and to set the terms of their loans.

Amended and Restated Agreement

This is a new venture debt agreement that supersedes and replaces the original agreement. The new agreement might have new terms or changes to existing terms, and both parties must sign it for it to be effective.

Amortization

the process of paying off a loan over time through regular payments that include both principal and interest. Venture debt may have a flexible amortization schedule, allowing borrowers to make smaller payments during the early stages of their business and larger payments as their cash flow increases.

Anti-dilution protection

a clause in a venture debt agreement that protects the lender's equity stake in the borrower's company. If the company issues new shares at a lower price than the lender paid, the lender may receive additional shares or a cash payment as compensation.

Asset-based lending

a type of venture debt where loans are secured by a borrower's assets, such as inventory or accounts receivable. It allows companies to borrow money based on their assets rather than their cash flow or creditworthiness. This type of financing is often used by companies with seasonal or cyclical businesses.

Assignment

the transfer of a venture debt agreement from one lender to another. Assignments may occur when a lender sells its interest in the loan to a third party or when a borrower refinances its debt with a new lender.

Attack loan

a type of venture debt that is secured by the borrower's equity or assets. Attack loans are high-risk, high-reward investments that may offer a substantial return if the borrower is successful, but may also result in a complete loss of investment.

Availment

a term used in venture debt to describe the process of accessing funds from a line of credit or loan. Availment may be done in increments, based on the borrower's needs, and may be subject to certain conditions or restrictions.

Back-Ended Warrants

Back-Ended Warrants are a type of financial instrument that is used in conjunction with Venture Debt. These warrants are typically issued to the lender during the loan process and provide the lender with the right to purchase the startup's equity in the future at a fixed price. Back-ended warrants are usually exercised after a certain milestone has been achieved, such as a successful exit or a Series B funding round. Back-ended warrants provide lenders with a potential upside in the event of a successful exit or liquidity event.

Backup Management

A plan devised by companies to prepare for potential operational or financial difficulties in the future. For venture debt, establishing a backup management plan can help ensure timely repayment of the loan in the event of unexpected financial downturns.

Balance Sheet

 A financial statement that presents the company's financial position at a specific point in time. It includes assets, liabilities, and equity. In venture debt, balance sheet fortification can be necessary to maintain financial stability and creditworthiness.

Balloon Payment

A Balloon payment is a large payment that is due at the end of a loan term. It is used in Venture Debt to offer smaller monthly payments and to lessen the cash flow burden on a startup. However, the balloon payment is due at the end of the loan term, which can create a significant cash flow burden for a startup if they are not prepared. This payment is usually higher than the monthly payments and is intended to be repaid from the proceeds of a successful exit or refinancing.

Bank Covenants

Bank Covenants are a set of terms and conditions that are included in Venture Debt agreements. These covenants are meant to protect the lender and typically include things like debt ratios, cash flow requirements, and other financial metrics. Bank covenants are designed to ensure that the borrower maintains certain levels of financial stability and meet their loan repayment obligations. Failure to comply with bank covenants can have serious consequences, including default on the loan and the acceleration of the payment of the entire loan amount.

Bankruptcy

A legal status in which a company is declared unable to pay off its debts. This can have serious implications for both the company and its investors. For venture debt, it is essential that companies maintain their ability to make payments on time and avoid bankruptcy.

Board of Directors

Individuals elected to oversee and govern the management team of a company. In venture debt, the board of directors can play an important role in creating strategies for financial management, optimizing cash flow, and overall business growth.

Borrowing Base

Borrowing Base refers to the maximum amount of money that a borrower can draw from a Venture Debt facility. The Borrowing Base is determined by the value of the borrower's assets, which usually consist of accounts receivable, inventory, and equipment. The lender usually sets a percentage on the appraised value of these assets, which determines the maximum amount the borrower can borrow. Monitoring of the Borrowing Base is done regularly and can result in an adjustment in the amount of credit available to the borrower.

Borrowing Base Certificate

A document that shows the value of a business's assets that can be used as collateral for a loan or venture debt. The certificate helps the lender determine the collateral value for the venture debt and reduces the risk associated with the loan.

Break-even Analysis

Break-even analysis is the process of determining the point at which a startup becomes profitable in Venture Debt. This usually involves calculating the total cost of running the business, including salaries, overheads and other expenses. The analysis also involves calculating the revenue necessary to cover the costs and determining at what point the business is profitable. Break-even analysis is important for Venture Debt because it helps investors determine the viability of the startup and whether or not to extend them credit.

Bridge Financing

Bridge Financing is a form of Venture Debt that helps startups get through a financial gap between funding rounds. It is a short-term debt that is extended to a startup, usually in the form of a loan or a convertible note. This type of financing is attractive to early-stage startups because it generally comes with less dilution than equity financing. Typically, bridge loans are used to fund growth, working capital requirements or to meet immediate cash requirements. It is important to note that bridge financing usually has a higher interest rate than regular loans and may include additional fees.

Bridging Loan

A short-term loan provided to a company to cover the period between two financing rounds. These loans are typically used to bridge financing gaps and maintain smooth operations in the company. In venture debt, bridging loans can provide immediate funding for the company's upcoming capital expenditures.

Building Relationships

A crucial aspect of venture debt wherein the lender establishes a long-term relationship with the company. Building relationships helps both parties understand the needs of the other, leading to better terms, conditions, and rates for the venture debt.

Bullet Loan

Bullet Loan refers to a type of loan that is repaid with a lump sum payment at the end of the loan term. This type of loan is usually short-term and has a set maturity date. In Venture Debt, Bullet loans usually have a higher interest rate than traditional loans and can be used to finance working capital or growth-related expenses. One of the benefits of a Bullet Loan is that it can help reduce the monthly payment burden on a startup. However, it is important to note that the final payment can be larger than the actual loan amount.

Bullet Repayment

A financing model where the borrower pays back the entire principal amount along with accumulated interest in a single lump-sum payment, typically at the end of the loan tenure. This model is commonly used in venture debt as it helps reduce the overall cost of borrowing by removing interest payments in the middle of the tenure.

Burn Rate

Burn Rate is the rate at which a startup is spending its cash in Venture Debt. It refers to the monthly amount of money that is being spent to keep the business running, such as covering salaries, overheads, and other expenses. Burn Rate is important to Venture Debt because it helps investors determine how much credit to extend a startup based on their ability to maintain a positive cash flow.

Business Development

The process of identifying and targeting potential customers for a product or service. For venture debt, business development strategies can help improve a company's cash flow and revenue growth, and consequently, maximize the chances of loan repayment success.

Business Models

The way in which a company creates, delivers, and captures value. In venture debt, understanding the business model is important when assessing the viability of the investment, the repayment capacity, and the overall financial health of the company.

Business Plan

Business Plan refers to a comprehensive document which outlines a startup's objectives and strategies in Venture Debt. It should include a detailed description of the company, its products or services, target market, competitive landscape, financial projections, and operating plan. A business plan is important in Venture Debt because it helps investors determine the viability of a startup and whether it is worth investing in.

Buyout Financing

Buyout Financing refers to a form of Venture Debt that is used to finance the acquisition of a company by another company. This type of financing is usually structured as a loan, and the purchase price of the company is used as collateral. Buyout Financing is important in Venture Debt, as it can help companies take advantage of acquisition opportunities without diluting the equity of the company. It also allows the acquiring company to leverage the assets of the company being acquired.

Call Option

A financial instrument that gives the holder the right, but not the obligation, to buy an asset at a predetermined price at a specified time in the future. Often included as a right for the lender in venture debt transactions if the start-up breaches certain covenants or fails to adhere to loan terms.

Cap Table

A record of all the shareholders in a company, their ownership percentage, and the capitalization of the company. An accurate cap table is critical in maintaining transparency and fairness when raising additional capital, granting equity incentives, and when exiting the company.

Capital Expenditure

Any expense incurred that is deemed to be a strategic long-term investment, such as the purchase of a new manufacturing plant or development of a new product. Venture debt can allow start-ups to undertake capital expenditures without giving up equity to finance the purchase.

Cash Flow Positive

A situation where a company generates more cash inflows than outflows during a given period. This provides the company with a firmer financial footing and increases its ability to repay debt obligations. Venture debt can help start-ups become cash flow positive by providing the capital to bridge the gap between revenue and capital expenditure.

Clean Tech

A term used to describe start-ups that develop and produce renewable energy, energy efficiency, or environmentally sustainable products. Clean Tech start-ups often require large-scale capital investments and venture debt can provide an essential financing option for scaling up their operations.

Collateral

Security pledged for a loan, which can be taken over by the lender in case the borrower fails to repay the loan. In venture debt, it can be a wide range of assets, including intellectual property or equity. Collateral can be a valuable negotiating tool in securing advantageous loan terms with lenders.

Commercialization

The process of bringing a product or service to market, including acquiring regulatory approvals, securing distribution channels, and launching marketing campaigns. Commercialization is a capital-intensive process for startups and often necessitates a combination of equity and venture debt capital.

Contingent Remuneration

Interest and fees payable only upon the happening of certain contingencies or events, such as the borrower's exit or successful conversion of debt to equity. Often used in venture debt instruments to align the interests of the borrower and lender.

Convertible Notes

A type of debt instrument that can convert into equity at a later stage. This is a flexible way to raise money and delay setting a valuation. Convertible notes are very popular in the venture industry, as investors are comfortable with investing in startups that are still too young to have a valuation.

Covenant

A promise made by the borrower to the lender regarding certain actions or limitations on its behavior. A popular type of covenant in venture debt is the restriction on the borrower from securing extra financing or selling equity to other investors without the approval of the lender.

Debenture

A type of unsecured bond that is backed only by the issuer's creditworthiness, rather than collateral. In venture debt, debentures may be issued as a form of subordinated debt, providing lenders with a higher yield in exchange for a lower priority in the capital structure.

Debt covenant

A contractual agreement between a borrower and lender that sets limits on the borrower's actions, such as restrictions on dividend payments or debt issuance. In venture debt, lenders may impose covenants to mitigate risk and protect their investment.

Debt funding

The act of raising capital by borrowing money from lenders, rather than issuing equity to investors. In venture debt, debt funding can provide companies with an alternative to equity financing, allowing them to preserve ownership and control while still accessing capital.

Debt maturity

The date when a loan or bond must be repaid in full, including all interest and principal payments. In venture debt, loan maturities can vary from a few months to several years, depending on the lender's risk appetite and the borrower's needs.

Debt refinancing

The act of replacing one or more existing loans or bonds with new debt, often at a lower interest rate or longer maturity. In venture debt, refinancing can be used to lower the cost of capital and improve cash flow, while also providing investors with a more attractive risk and return profile.

Debt service coverage ratio

A measure of a company's ability to meet its interest and principal payments on debt, calculated by dividing its cash flow by its debt service. In venture debt, lenders typically require a debt service coverage ratio of at least 1.2

Debt-to-equity ratio

A metric used by lenders to evaluate a company's risk profile, calculated by dividing its total debt by its total equity. In venture debt, lenders typically prefer a debt-to-equity ratio of no more than 1

Default

A failure to meet the terms of a loan agreement, such as missing a payment or breaching a financial covenant. In venture debt, a default can trigger a range of consequences, including legal action, foreclosure, and loss of control over the company.

Dilution

The decrease in the percentage of ownership held by existing shareholders when new equity is issued. In venture debt, dilution can occur when convertible notes are converted to equity, reducing the share of the company held by its founders and early investors.

Drawdown

The act of borrowing funds from a credit facility, such as a line of credit or revolver. In venture debt, drawdowns are often used to fund working capital, equipment purchases, or growth initiatives.

Early-stage companies

Refers to newly founded companies or companies that are operating in their early stages. Such companies lack a stable cash flow and may require capital injections to help them grow. For venture debt investors, early-stage companies are a high-risk investment opportunity.

Enterprise value

Refers to the total value of a company that includes its equity value and its debt value. For venture debt, it signifies the total value of an organization in which venture debt investors have invested.

Equity dilution

The reduction of an individual's ownership in a company when new shares are issued. Equity dilution is a common occurrence when a company needs additional funding, such as in venture debt financing. When additional equity is issued for venture debt financing, the company's founders' ownership percentage dilutes.

Equity kicker

A term used in venture debt, which refers to an additional equity option that investors can hold on to. Venture debt investors may choose to convert their debt and get a small amount of additional equity in a company. Equity kickers are cheaper than buying additional equity through regular means and offer investors additional upside.

Equity value

The value of a company's assets that remain after all its debts and liabilities have been paid off. For venture debt, equity value represents the worth of a company that entrepreneurs may offer to their investors to convert their debt into equity.

Escrow account

A bank account set up to hold funds or assets during various transactions, including venture debt transactions. Escrow accounts ensure that proper procedures are in place to distribute the funds or assets.

Event of default

A term used in venture debt contracts. This is when the borrower violates the loan's covenants or fails to repay the loan. In such situations, lenders are within their rights to demand immediate repayment of the entire loan amount.

Exit strategy

Refers to strategies companies use to sell or liquidate their investments. For venture debt investors, exit strategies could be through secondary sales or IPOs. A robust and successful exit strategy is incredibly important to venture debt investors, and it enables them to calculate their potential returns.

Extension fees

Refer to fees that borrowers pay to extend their venture debt duration. Since venture debt loans have a specific timeline, companies can request an extension for additional time to repay the loan. Extension fees help lenders cover for the additional interest they may lose while extending the loan duration.

Face Value

Face value is a term used to describe the initial value of a security or asset when it is issued. The term is commonly used in the context of stock, bonds, or promissory notes. Venture capitalists may look at the face value of the securities issued by companies before investing in them. It represents the nominal value of an investment before any additional fees or costs.

Face-Term Ratio

Face-term ratio refers to the comparison of the outstanding principal payment of a loan and the maturity date. It is common in venture debt and shows the proportion of principal payment the borrower must repay before the due date. Venture capitalists may look at the face-term ratio when evaluating investment opportunities in companies.

Financial Covenants

A financial covenant is a financial agreement between a lender and a borrower, setting the terms and conditions for loan repayment. The covenant requires the borrower to meet specific financial criteria or promises to maintain certain ratios or conditions. For instance, the lender may require the borrower to maintain a specific cash flow or a profit margin. Venture capitalists may require companies to maintain financial covenants in certain situations.

First Lien Debt

This is a type of secured debt where the lender has the first claim to the collateral in case of a default. It gives the lender priority over other obligations that might be owed to other creditors. Thus, first-lien debt is less risky for lenders, and they may offer lower interest rates when it is used as a means of funding.

Fixed Interest Rate

It is a type of rate that remains constant throughout the life of a debt or loan. Fixed rates are beneficial to borrowers as they provide stability, and the borrower can make prior calculations on the amount of interest they should expect in the future. Venture debt may offer fixed interest rates for companies seeking funding.

Floating Interest Rate

It is a type of interest rate that fluctuates based on prevailing market rates. This can be beneficial to lenders as they can take advantage of the rising rates. However, borrowers may face difficulties as they will have to pay more interest if rates go up. Venture debt may offer floating interest rates that utilize a market index as a benchmark.

Founder Friendly

A term that is gaining traction in venture capital is "Founder Friendly." It is a reminder that the venture capitalist is there to support the growth of the company and not to dictate the future of the business. Venture debt may be tailored to be founder-friendly, keeping the founders' interests and rights in mind while providing the required funding.

Four Stages of Venture Debt

The four stages of venture debt include early, middle, later, and pre-IPO. Each phase represents the stage of the company's growth and also the level of risk involved. At the early stage, venture capital may require more equity before lending. At the Pre-IPO stage, companies may look to finance their debts through strategic partnerships with lenders.

Fundable Debt-to-Equity Ratio

This is a metric that compares the amount of debt to the amount of equity that a venture capitalist is willing to provide. It represents the proportion of debt capital that a company can take on without risking the equity provided by the investors. Venture capitalists may look at this ratio when evaluating investment opportunities in companies.

Funded Debt

This is a type of debt where the borrower needs to payback borrowed amount with interest. It is secured by an asset, and in case of a default, the lender can seize the asset to recover the outstanding amount. Funded debt is the opposite of unfunded debt, where there is no collateral or asset tied to the borrowed money. When venture capitalists invest in a company, they can provide funded debt to such businesses.

Gearing ratio

This is the ratio of a company's total debt to its equity. It's used to assess the financial leverage of a company and its ability to meet its debt obligations. A high gearing ratio may indicate that a company is more vulnerable to financial distress, making it a riskier investment opportunity.

Goodwill

This is an intangible asset that represents the excess of the purchase price over the fair value of identifiable assets acquired in a business combination. Goodwill can arise from synergies between businesses, brand recognition, intellectual property, and other factors that contribute to the overall value of a company.

Grace period

This is a period of time during which a borrower is not required to make payments on a loan. Grace periods can be useful for a borrower who needs time to establish financial stability before beginning to make loan payments. During the grace period, interest may still accrue, adding to the total cost of the loan.

Gross margin

This is the percentage of revenue remaining after the cost of goods sold has been deducted. Gross margin is often used as an indicator of a company's efficiency in managing its operations, as a higher gross margin typically indicates better cost control and pricing power.

Gross revenue

This is the total revenue earned by a company before any deductions are made for expenses or taxes. Gross revenue is rarely used as a measure of a company's financial performance, as it does not take into account the costs of operating the business.

Growth capital

This refers to funds provided to a company that is growing and requires capital to expand its operations. Growth capital is often used to finance investments in new markets or product lines, or in research and development activities aimed at improving a company's competitiveness.

Growth equity

This refers to investments made in companies that are expanding and require capital to accelerate their growth. Growth equity investments are typically made in companies that are generating significant revenue and have a proven business model, but require additional funds to reach their full potential.

Growth-stage companies

Large, established companies with a proven business model and revenue streams that are looking for capital to accelerate growth. These companies have typically moved beyond the start-up phase and require additional funds to fuel their expansion plans.

Guarantee

This is a formal promise or pledge made by a borrower to a lender to repay a debt. Guarantees can be given by an individual or a company, and can offer additional security to a lender by providing a source of repayment in the event of default.

Guaranteed securities

These are securities that are backed by a guarantee from another party, such as a government agency or a bank. The guarantee provides additional security for the investor, as it assures that the investor will receive full repayment of the security even in the event of default by the issuer. Guaranteed securities are often used in low-risk investment portfolios for their added security.

Haircut

A haircut is a reduction in the value of an asset or security. In the context of venture debt, haircut may refer to the potential loss of value that lenders may face if a portfolio company defaults on its debt obligations or experiences a downturn in its business.

Hidden covenants

Hidden covenants refer to conditions or requirements that are not explicitly stated in a loan agreement, but rather are implied or understood between the lender and borrower. These covenants may dictate the behavior or actions of the borrower, and failure to comply with them may result in default or other penalties. Venture debt may include hidden covenants as a way for lenders to protect their investment or to ensure that the borrower meets certain performance milestones.

Hidden warrants

Hidden warrants refer to equity options that are embedded in debt securities. These warrants may be "hidden" because they are not explicitly stated or disclosed in the terms of the debt, but rather are included as a component of the overall investment. Venture debt may include hidden warrants as a way for lenders to participate in the future value of a portfolio company.

High-water mark

A high-water mark is the highest point that an asset or investment has achieved. In the context of venture debt, lenders may use a high-water mark as a benchmark for future performance, allowing them to participate in the potential upside of a portfolio company if its value exceeds previous levels.

High-yield debt

High-yield debt refers to debt securities with lower credit ratings than investment-grade bonds. These bonds are also known as "junk bonds" and usually offer higher yields to investors to compensate for the increased risk. Venture debt may fall into the category of high-yield debt because it is often extended to startups or companies with less established credit profiles.

Holdco facility

A holdco facility is a type of financing arrangement in which a holding company secures a loan that can be used to fund the operations of its subsidiaries. In the context of venture debt, a holdco facility may be used to provide additional capital to a portfolio company while minimizing the dilution of existing equity holders.

Holding period

Holding period refers to the length of time that an investor holds a particular security or asset. In the context of venture debt, holding periods may be shorter than those of traditional long-term investments because the loans are generally structured with specific repayment timelines or convertible features.

Horizon analysis

Horizon analysis is a valuation technique that evaluates the future cash flows of an investment over a specific time horizon. In the context of venture debt, horizon analysis may be used to assess the potential returns of a debt investment in a startup or growth-stage company.

Hybrid structure

A hybrid structure refers to a financing arrangement that combines elements of both debt and equity. In the context of venture debt, a hybrid structure may involve raising funds through a combination of traditional bank loans (debt) and convertible securities (equity). This structure allows companies to raise capital without diluting ownership too much, and may be particularly useful for growth-stage companies that have already raised some equity capital but need additional funds to continue expanding.

Indebtedness

The total amount of debt owed by a company. In venture debt, the lender will typically require regular financial reporting to monitor the company's level of indebtedness relative to its ability to repay the loan.

Inflation

The rate at which the general level of prices for goods and services is rising, and subsequently, purchasing power is falling. In the context of venture debt, inflation can erode the value of the loan over time, leading to a decrease in repayment value.

Insolvency

The state of being unable to pay debts as they come due. In venture debt, insolvency may occur if the start-up company cannot generate sufficient revenue or raise additional funding to repay the loan. Depending on the terms of the loan agreement, insolvency may trigger a default and result in legal action by the lender.

Installment Payments

Repayment of a loan in a series of fixed payments, typically made at regular intervals over the life of the loan. In venture debt, installment payments may be structured to coincide with the company's cash flow, with larger payments due when the company is expected to have higher cash balances.

Interest Coverage Ratio

A financial ratio used to measure a company's ability to pay interest on its debt. In venture debt, a high interest coverage ratio is desirable as it indicates that the company's cash flow is sufficient to meet its borrowing obligations.

Interest Rate

The cost of borrowing money from a lender expressed as a percentage of the principal amount borrowed. In the context of venture debt, the interest rate charged is usually higher than traditional bank loans to reflect the higher risk inherent in lending to start-up companies.

Investment Grade

A credit rating indicating that a particular debt security is likely to be repaid. In venture debt, start-up companies are typically not considered investment grade borrowers due to their higher risk profile.

Investment Horizon

The length of time an investor plans to hold an investment before selling it. In venture debt, lenders typically have a shorter investment horizon than equity investors, and the repayment schedule of the loan is structured accordingly.

Investor Syndicate

A group of investors who collectively provide funding to a start-up company. In venture debt, the lender may require a start-up to have an investor syndicate in place as a condition of the loan, as it demonstrates a level of support and confidence in the company's future success.

IPO

Initial Public Offering. The first time that a company's shares are sold to the public, typically on a stock exchange. In venture debt, lenders may include IPO-related covenants in the loan agreement, in which the company agrees to certain actions or restrictions related to going public.

J-Curve

The J-curve is a model that describes the expected financial returns of a company that has been invested in through venture capital. It largely depicts the notion that the investment value will dip or remain low after the initial investment is made, followed by an upward climb as the investment's value increases exponentially. As the investment begins to bear fruits, the returns start to surpass the amount that was invested initially, showing the investor a significant return on investment.

Job Creation

This term refers to the number of jobs that can be expected to be created in a company due to venture capital investment. This return on investment is a key consideration for venture capitalists as their investment not only helps the company involved but often also provides jobs and boosts local economies.

Joint Creditor

A joint creditor is a collection of lenders whose debt overlaps or is of an identical nature. In venture debt, this might consist of investors who have given money to the same emerging company.

Junior Debt

Junior debt is a type of venture debt that is considered subordinate to senior debt. Junior debt is typically higher in interest rates than senior debt as it is perceived as riskier. When a company defaults on their payments, senior lenders will be paid first and whatever amount remaining will be then used to pay back junior lenders.

Junior Debt Investor

A junior debt investor is an individual or entity that provides junior debt financing to a company. Junior debt investors usually receive higher returns compared to senior debt investors, but the risk of not being repaid might be higher in case of a company defaulting on its payments. Unlike equity investors, junior debt investors don't have ownership rights in the company.

Junior Lien

Junior lien holders have the right to the collateral that is supporting a loan but are only paid after the senior lien holder is paid. Being lower in priority, junior liens are generally considered more risky, meaning that they come with higher interest rates than senior liens.

Junior Note

Junior notes are also subordinate to senior debt or other debt instruments. Here, the junior note is typically paid after senior debt payments have been made. For this reason, junior notes come with higher interest rates than their senior counterparts.

Junior Security

In venture debt, a junior security refers to a security that has a lower claim over assets compared to another security, referred to as the senior security. In the case where a company defaults on payments, the junior security holders are paid only if senior security holders are paid in full. Junior securities come with higher interest rates as a result of the increased risk.

Junior Tranche

A junior tranche refers to a distinct portion of a secured loan that is junior to another loan portion, i.e. a senior tranche. In this type of financing structure, the junior tranche will only receive payment if there's enough money remaining after the senior tranche has been paid in full. This tranche typically comes with a higher interest rate due to the higher risk involved.

Junk Bonds

Junk bonds refer to high-yield bonds offered to investors by companies with a lower credit rating. These types of bonds come with a high risk for investors, which makes them a popular choice for venture capitalists. This investment also offers a high reward option for investors willing to take on the higher risk with interest rates at times exceeding the double digits.

Keepwell agreement

A keepwell agreement is a legal document where the parent company or an affiliate of a borrower agrees to provide financial support to the borrower if they are unable to maintain their debt obligations to the lender. It is essentially a guarantee in the form of a contract that shows the borrower has a strong financial backing.

Kernel of value

This refers to the core value proposition of a business that makes it unique and valuable to its customers. Venture debt lenders will evaluate the kernel of value when assessing a company's potential for success and may provide financing based on that value.

Key covenant

An important clause in venture debt agreements that outlines the terms and conditions of the loan including repayment schedule, interest, and collateral. This covenant typically includes financial ratios and other performance metrics that the borrower must meet to avoid defaulting on the loan.

K-factor

The K-factor is a measure of a company's growth rate and is used as a basis for determining the appropriate loan amount for venture debt financing. This measure takes into account a company's revenue growth rate, operating margins, and other financial factors.

Kickers

This refers to additional returns or benefits that a venture debt lender may receive if the borrower meets certain performance targets. Kickers are often used to incentivize borrowers to perform well and can include equity warrants or other types of equity participation in the business.

Kiosk financing

This is a term used to describe venture debt financing that focuses on businesses that provide automated retail solutions such as vending machines, self-service kiosks, and other automated sales channels. Kiosk financing lenders evaluate businesses based on their potential customer base, location, and other factors that determine their likelihood of success.

Knockout clause

This is a legal provision in venture debt agreements that allows the lender to demand full repayment of the loan if the borrower violates a key covenant or fails to meet certain performance targets. The knockout clause is often used by lenders to protect against excessive risk and to ensure that borrowers meet their obligations under the loan agreement.

Knowledge-based lending

Knowledge-based lending is a type of venture debt financing that focuses on intellectual property and innovative technologies. This type of financing is often used by biotech and life science startups that rely heavily on their intellectual property to create value.

Known issues

This is a term used when referring to factors that may negatively impact a borrower's ability to repay a loan, such as pending litigation, regulatory issues, or other challenges. Lenders will evaluate known issues as part of their risk assessment process and may include special provisions or higher interest rates to account for the increased risks.

KPIs

Key Performance Indicators (KPIs) are measurable data points that show how well a business is performing. Venture debt lenders often use KPIs to evaluate the financial health of a business before approving a loan. Common KPIs include revenue growth, operating margin, and customer acquisition cost.

Late Payment Fee

A late payment fee is a financial penalty imposed on a borrower or startup for making a payment after the due date. Late payment fees are a common feature in venture debt financing to encourage prompt loan repayment and to cover the cost of monitoring and managing loans.

Lender-To-Marketplace Funding

This refers to a financing method where a lender provides funds to an online marketplace that, in turn, lends the money to borrowers. This method is sometimes used in venture debt financing, allowing lenders to extend loans to startups more easily.

Leverage

Leverage refers to the amount of debt a startup has relative to its equity. High leverage can amplify returns or losses and is a crucial component in venture debt financing. Lenders typically prefer startups with low levels of leverage.

Lien

A lien is a legal claim or encumbrance that a lender places on a borrower's asset (e.g., property, equity). In venture debt financing, lenders often require liens on a startup's assets to mitigate risk and ensure repayment.

Liquidation Preference

This term describes the order in which a company's assets are distributed to various investors if the company goes bankrupt or is sold. Investors who have higher liquidation preferences will receive priority in asset distribution. In venture debt financing, the liquidation preference can have a significant impact on the returns for both investors and lenders.

Loan Amortization

Loan amortization refers to the process of paying off a loan over time, typically through regular payments that include both interest and principal. It's an essential component of venture debt financing to ensure timely repayment.

Loan Covenant

A loan covenant is a provision in a loan agreement that outlines the rights and obligations of the borrower and lender. Covenants are used to set certain restrictions and requirements on the borrower, such as maintaining a certain level of cash reserves or limiting additional borrowing.

Loan Structure

The loan structure is the specific details of a loan agreement, including the interest rate, repayment period, and other key terms. Loan structure is a critical component of venture debt financing, as it determines the business' ability to repay the loan and the lender's potential returns.

Loan-To-Value Ratio

The Loan-to-Value Ratio (LTV) is a common metric used in venture debt financing to determine how much debt a lender can provide in relation to the value of the asset (usually a startup's equity). LTV is calculated by dividing the loan amount by the asset value.

Lock-Up Period

A lock-up period is a period of time in which an investor or lender is restricted from selling or transferring their securities or assets. In venture debt financing, a lock-up period may be imposed on the startup or lender to ensure stability and meet certain goals.

Negative covenant

This is a clause in venture debt agreements that prohibit a borrower from performing certain actions that could impede their ability to repay the loan. Examples include limitations on issuing new debt, restrictions on the issuance of dividends, and restrictions on the sale of assets necessary for the company's operations.

Negative pledge

In venture debt, a negative pledge is a pledge by the borrower not to grant any security interests in their assets to other lenders. Its aim is to protect the lender from subordinated liens on the borrower's assets. It can raise the lender's comfort level in lending and ensure seniority in claim if the borrower faces financial difficulties.

Net income margin

It is the percentage of revenue that remains after all expenses have been deducted, including interest expenses from loans. In venture debt, a company can use the net income margin to determine how much they can afford to borrow, and lenders can use it to determine how much they can lend to the company.

Non-compete agreement

A non-compete agreement requires the borrower to refrain from working for or starting a business in the same industry as the lender for a specific period after the loan has been paid. In venture debt, lenders may require that borrowers sign a non-compete agreement to protect their interests in the borrower's intellectual property.

Non-dilutive financing

It is a form of financing that does not require an equity stake from the lender. In venture debt, companies can obtain non-dilutive capital that enables them to maintain their ownership stake in the business while still gaining access to additional capital.

Nondisclosure agreement (NDA)

An NDA is a legally binding document that prevents the recipient of confidential information from disclosing it to others. In venture debt, NDAs are used when lenders and borrowers share sensitive information during the due diligence process.

Non-monetary default

This is a type of debt default that does not involve the borrower's inability to make payments. Rather, it results from breaches of non-financial obligations by the borrower such as failure in providing an audited financial statement, failure to maintain adequate levels of insurance, and regulatory breaches.

Non-recourse loan

It is a type of loan where the lender only has rights to the collateral in the event of a default, and cannot go after the borrower's other assets. For venture debt, the lender may only recoup the value of the collateral (such as IP or equipment) if there is a default.

Non-warrantable investments

These are investments that the lender or the underwriter cannot sell, resell or refinance because the investment doesn't meet the lender's or underwriter's requirements. Examples of non-warrantable investments include condos that are investment properties, vacation homes, and properties located in distress areas.

Notice

A notice is a formal announcement or communication used in venture debt to inform a party of a specific condition, development, or action. It is commonly used in relation to events of default, amendments to loan terms, and other material changes to the borrower's or lender's obligations.

Participation

In venture debt, the term participation is referred to the right of the lender to participate in a subsequent equity round, alongside the equity investors.

Payment Terms

Payment terms refer to the predetermined schedule according to which the principal and interest are to be repaid. It is a crucial aspect of venture debt as it determines the amount of cash outflow required by the business.

Personal Guarantee

Personal Guarantee is a pledge by a borrower that they will personally repay the loan if the business fails to repay. It's often required while taking venture debt as startups are often unproven, and lenders need a backup plan in case of default.

Placement Agent

A placement agent is a financial intermediary that helps the borrower to secure venture debt financing by finding potential investors for them.

Prepayment Penalty

It is a fee charged by lenders for repaying the debt before its due date. In case of early repayment, the lender loses out on the interest payment that would have accrued, and hence the prepayment penalty is charged.

Prime Rate

The prime rate is the interest rate that banks charge their most creditworthy customers. It is an important benchmark to determine the interest rates charged for venture debt financing.

Principal Amount

The amount borrowed by the borrower from the lender is known as the principal amount. In venture debt, it's the amount that a startup raises in the form of debt, to be repaid with interest over a specific period.

Profitability

Lenders offering venture debt typically look for businesses that are profitable, have a proven business model, and require debt capital to drive growth. Profitability is an important factor for lenders as it ensures that the business will have the ability to repay the debt.

Publicity

While taking venture debt, businesses are often required to disclose information regarding the debt and the terms of the deal to the public. This is known as publicity, and it helps in establishing credibility with potential investors.

Purchase Order Financing

Purchase order financing is a type of venture debt that allows a business to borrow funds to pay the supplier for the cost of goods necessary to fulfill a customer's order. This financing option helps businesses that have insufficient working capital to pay for the inventory necessary to fulfill larger client orders.

Qualification amount

The qualification amount is the maximum amount of venture debt that a lender is willing to provide to a startup. This amount is generally determined by the lender's assessment of the startup's cash flow, creditworthiness, and projected growth. Qualification amount can be an important consideration for entrepreneurs when evaluating different lenders and their ability to meet their capital requirements.

Qualified financing round

A qualified financing round is an equity financing event in which investors collectively inject a certain amount of capital into a startup. Qualified financing rounds are significant because they often trigger the conversion of convertible debt into equity, as well as provide a new valuation for the company. These rounds are also used by venture debt lenders to determine whether to continue to fund a startup and the terms of such funding.

Qualifying criteria

These are the conditions that an entrepreneur must meet to receive venture debt funding. Qualifying criteria may vary from lender to lender, but generally include requirements such as a certain amount of revenue or a proven track record of growth. Entrepreneurs should familiarize themselves with the qualifying criteria of different lenders to increase their chances of securing funding.

Quarterly interest

Venture debt loans generally have quarterly interest payments, unlike traditional bank loans which have monthly payments. Quarterly interest can provide entrepreneurs with more cash flow to invest on other critical areas of their business. However, entrepreneurs must plan their finances accordingly to ensure they have sufficient cash to meet their quarterly interest obligation.

Quartile

In venture capital, quartile refers to the ranking of funds based on their performance compared to other funds in the same category. Top-performing funds are generally placed in the first quartile, while the worst-performing funds are placed in the fourth quartile. Quartile rankings are an essential metric for limited partners who use them to evaluate and make decisions on investment opportunities.

Query

Query refers to the process of asking questions about a startup's financial health and cash flow. Venture debt lenders often use this process to determine the funding amount, interest rates, and other terms of financing. Queries are also used to evaluate a startup's potential risks and establish contingencies to mitigate these risks.

Quick-decision funding

Venture debt lenders can provide quick-decision funding compared to other types of financing such as equity. This is because lenders focus on the borrower's cash flow and business model rather than the entrepreneur's personal credit history or collateral. Quick-decision funding can be beneficial for entrepreneurs who need capital quickly to capitalize on an opportunity or manage a short-term cash flow issue.

Quiet amendment

A quiet amendment is a modification to the terms of the loan or credit agreement that does not require public disclosure. This type of amendment is often used to address minor or technical issues with the loan, such as adjusting the interest rate or changing the payment schedule. Quiet amendments are generally more straightforward and less time-consuming than other types of amendments, such as amendments that require lender approval or significant changes to the loan's terms.

Quiet period

A quiet period is a period when a company limits the flow of information about its financial health and activities. This is often in preparation for an IPO or merger. During the quiet period, a company's management cannot make public statements that can influence the company's stock price. This is designed to prevent insiders from taking advantage of privileged information or hype surrounding the company's upcoming activities.

Quorum

Quorum is the minimum number of investors required, either in person or by proxy, to conduct a valid vote on issues such as changes to the company's charter or bylaws. Quorums are set by default in a company's charter and can only be modified with a supermajority vote of the company's shareholders. Quorums are essential to ensure that decisions are made with the support of a critical mass of the company's stakeholders.

Repayment period

The repayment period is the timeframe within which a loan must be paid back. Lenders set up the repayment period to ensure that borrowers repay the money within a specific timeframe, and usually include pre-set repayment schedules and deadlines.

Research and development

Research and development refer to activities undertaken by a company to invent, create, or improve their products and services. Companies invest in R&D to stay ahead in the competitive market, improve the quality of their products, or to develop entirely new products to increase revenue.

Residual value

Residual value refers to the estimated value of an asset at the end of its useful life, after accounting for depreciation. Depreciation refers to the decline in an asset's value over time due to wear and tear or obsolescence.

Restrictive covenants

Restrictive covenants are requirements set by lenders to ensure that borrowers meet specific financial and operational requirements. The covenants could include conditions such as minimum revenue levels, debt-to-equity ratio or cash flow targets, and are put in place to protect the lender's interest.

Return on Investment (ROI)

Return on Investment (ROI) is a ratio that measures the profit or loss made on an investment relative to the amount of money invested. It is used to determine if an investment is worthwhile or not by comparing the amount earned to the initial investment.

Revolver

A revolver is a type of loan under which a borrower can access a set amount of financing over a certain period from a line of credit that is re-borrowable after it has been repaid. It allows the borrower to withdraw money when they need it and make repayments as required.

Revolving credit

Revolving credit is a financing agreement where the lender provides a line of credit for a specified amount, and the borrower can use and repay the credit as needed. The interest is charged only on the balance the borrower owes on the line of credit.

Risk-adjusted return

Risk-adjusted return reflects the amount of return an investor expects to earn after taking into account the investment's level of risk. Risk-adjusted return helps investors determine the quantity and quality of risk they are willing to undertake in exchange for the anticipated return.

Road show

A road show is a series of presentations given to potential investors by a company looking to raise capital. The purpose of the road show is to market the investment opportunity to potential investors, explaining the benefits of investing and answering questions.

Royalty financing

Royalty financing is a funding method in which investors provide capital to businesses for a share of future revenue. In return, the investor is entitled to a portion of the company's earnings or receives an agreed-upon percentage of the profits generated from a specific product or service.

Term

Term Loan

Underwriting

The process in which a lender evaluates a borrower's creditworthiness and ability to repay a loan; in venture debt, underwriting typically involves analyzing a company's financial statements, business model, and growth prospects.

Unfunded capital commitments

The amount of capital that a limited partner has committed to a venture capital fund but has not yet invested; in venture debt, lenders may take into account a borrower's unfunded capital commitments when assessing its financial strength and ability to repay loans.

Unit economics

The analysis of a company's revenue and costs on a per-unit basis; in venture debt, lenders may analyze a company's unit economics to assess its profitability and potential for growth.

Unitranche

A type of debt facility that combines senior and subordinated debt into a single loan with a single interest rate and payment schedule; this can simplify the financing process and reduce costs for borrowers.

Unsecured debt

A type of debt that is not backed by collateral; in venture debt, unsecured debt is often used for early-stage companies that do not have significant assets.

Upside participation

A feature of venture debt that allows lenders to participate in a company's future growth through equity warrants or convertible notes; this provides an additional return on investment and can help bridge the gap between debt and equity financing.

Use of proceeds

The specific purposes for which a borrower intends to use the funds raised through a loan or financing round; in venture debt, lenders may require detailed information about a company's use of proceeds to ensure that the funds are being used effectively and in accordance with the agreed-upon terms.

User base

The number of people or organizations that use a particular product or service; in venture debt, a company's user base can be a key indicator of its growth potential and viability.

Utilization

The percentage of a venture debt facility that is currently being used by a borrower; lenders may monitor utilization closely to ensure that the borrower is using the funds effectively and not exceeding the agreed-upon limits.

Valuation Cap

A term used in convertible debt financing that puts a ceiling on the valuation of the company when the debt converts to equity. The valuation cap ensures that early investors in the company are guaranteed a certain return on their investment.

Value-Add Lender

A venture lender that offers additional services beyond just debt financing, such as access to networks, strategic partnerships, and business advice. Value-add lenders are often sought by companies that are looking for strategic partners in addition to financing.

Venture Debt Covenants

The specific conditions and restrictions placed on the borrower by the lender to ensure compliance with the terms of the financing agreement. These covenants can include restrictions on how the borrower uses the funds, financial performance ratios that must be met, and limits on debt levels.

Venture Debt Drawdown

The process of accessing funds from a venture debt facility. The borrower can draw down funds to meet short-term cash needs or to finance specific capital expenditures or growth initiatives.

Venture Debt Financing

A type of debt financing that is often provided to early-stage startups and growing companies with high potential. Unlike traditional bank loans, venture debt financing is considered a riskier form of financing due to its higher interest rates and stricter repayment terms.

Venture Debt Funding Rounds

The rounds of financing that a company goes through to secure venture debt financing. These rounds are similar to equity financing rounds but involve the issuance of debt instead of equity.

Venture Debt Instrument

A financial instrument that represents the obligation of a borrower to repay the principal amount of the loan plus interest. Venture debt instruments can take the form of convertible notes, lines of credit, term loans, or other types of debt.

Venture Debt Terms

The specific terms and conditions of the venture debt financing agreement that outline the repayment schedule, interest rate, and other contractual obligations. These terms are often negotiated between the borrower and the lender and can vary depending on the stage and size of the company.

Venture Debt vs. Equity Financing

A comparison of two types of financing options available to startups and emerging companies. While equity financing involves the issuance of shares in exchange for capital, venture debt financing involves the issuance of debt that must be repaid with interest.

Venture Lender

A specialized lending firm that focuses on providing venture debt financing to high-growth startups and emerging companies. These lenders offer non-dilutive financing solutions that complement equity funding and provide an alternative source of capital for growth.

Waiver

A document that allows the lender to give up its rights to enforce specific clauses in the loan agreement. This might include late payment fees or other penalties if the borrower is experiencing financial difficulties.

Warrants

These are securities that give the holder an option to buy shares of a company at a specific price. Warrants are often offered along with venture debt to incentivize investors to provide capital.

Weighted Average Cost of Capital (WACC)

This is used to measure the cost of capital for a company taking into account the different sources of financing (equity, debt, etc). WACC is often used to determine if it is economically viable for a company to take on venture debt.

Winding-Up Order

This is a legal order directing a company to cease operations and liquidate all assets. Companies that fail to pay debts owed to creditors or default on their venture debt often receive winding-up orders.

Working Capital

Working capital refers to a company's ability to meet its short-term financial obligations. Venture debt can help provide working capital to startups, allowing them to fund operations and investments.

Working Capital Loan

A type of venture debt used by startups to fund operational expenses. Unlike traditional loans, working capital loans have shorter repayment schedules and are provided quickly.

Workout

A workout is an agreement between the lender and the borrower to restructure the loan agreement or repayment schedule. Workouts often occur when the borrower is struggling to make payments or meet other obligations.

Write-Off

This is when investors cancel a portion or all of a company's debt due to failure to make payments or other breaches of contract. Write-offs often occur in venture debt financing when investors are trying to minimize their losses.

Year-over-Year Growth

Year-over-Year Growth (YoY) is the measure of a company's growth rate on an annual basis. It is calculated as the percentage difference between the current year's financial data and that of the corresponding period of the preceding year. YoY is a valuable metric for businesses to evaluate their growth momentum over an extended period.

Yield

Yield is the profitability of an investment over a specific period, expressed as a percentage. In debt financing, the yield is the interest rate paid by the borrower to the lender. Venture debt funds earn yields primarily from the interest charged on the loans issued to companies.

Yield Curve

The Yield Curve refers to the graphical representation of the relationship between bond yields and their respective maturities. A yield curve enables investors to compare the overall market's expectation of future interest rates and the associated risks with investing in treasuries of similar maturity dates. The yield curve is a crucial metric for investors to evaluate an economy's health as it reflects market expectations of future growth, inflation, and monetary policy.

Yield Maintenance

Yield Maintenance is a provision in the loan agreement that requires the borrower to make whole any loss the lender incurs as a result of early payments. Yield maintenance is usually calculated as the net present value of the difference between the outstanding debt's contractual cash flows and the expected future cash flows at the time of prepayment.

Yield on Cost

Yield on Cost (YOC) is the yield an investor experiences on their initial investment, calculated by dividing the annual dividend payment by the original purchase price of the investment. YOC is an essential metric for long-term investors who want to monitor their investment's growth and overall profitability.

Yield Spread

Yield spread is the difference in yield between two types of debt securities or two securities with different maturities. For example, a treasury bond may have a lower yield spread than a corporate bond due to its lower credit risk. Yield spread is a critical metric for investors to evaluate the overall credit quality and risks associated with the investment.

Yield to Call

Yield to Call (YTC) is an appreciation of the total yield of a bond for its expected remaining life, assuming that the bond is called. YTC is calculated using the bond's call price rather than its par value that shows the actual yield that the investor could earn should the bond be called by the issuer.

Yield to Maturity

Yield to Maturity (YTM) is the total return anticipated on a bond investment if the investment is held until it avails maturity. The yield to maturity is mainly considered in bond valuation and is used to compare the expected returns of different investments.

Yield to Worst

Yield to Worst (YTW) is the lowest potential yield that an investor can expect when investing in a bond. It is usually a conservative estimate and accounts for the potential negative scenarios that might impact the bond's yield. YTW is crucial for investors who are more risk-averse and want to assess the bond's downside risks.

Young Companies

A young company is a business enterprise that has been recently established and has a short operational history. Young companies have a higher risk of failure due to many reasons like weak financials, limited access to funding, and inadequate management teams. Venture debt is well suited for young companies that aim to grow rapidly and require working capital while preserving equity for further organizational value.

www.ingramcontent.com/pod-product-compliance
Lightning Source LLC
Chambersburg PA
CBHW071030220526
45467CB00004B/1601